GROWING FIG TREES

The complete guide to growing Fig trees from propagation to harvesting

Davies Cheruiyot

GROWING FIG TREES

Copyright © 2024 Davies Cheruiyot

All rights reserved.

CONTENTS

Acknowledgments

1 **GROWING FIGS**

   Introduction

   Benefits

2 **FIG TREE VARIETIES**

   Black Mission Figs

   Celeste Fig Trees

   Common Fig Tree

   Kadota Fig Trees

   Moreton Bay Fig Trees

   Chicago Hardy Fig Trees

   Indian Banyan Fig Trees

   Red Leaf Fig Trees

   Weeping Fig Trees

   Rubber Tree Fig Trees

   Fiddleleaf Fig Trees

   Chinese Banyan Fig Trees

Creeping Fig Trees

3 FIG TREE GROWING REQUIREMENTS

Light and Temperature

Soil

Propagation

Planting

Fertilizer

Water

Mulching

Repotting

Pruning

Harvesting

4 POPULAR FIG TREES PESTS AND DISEASES

Root Knot Nematodes

Spider Mites

Scales

Fruit Flies

Rust

Mealybugs

Thrips

Anthracnose

Root Rot

ACKNOWLEDGMENTS

I would like to express my gratitude to all people who helped me in editing and finalizing the final draft of this book.

1 GROWING FIGS

Introduction

Figs are deciduous trees from the family of Moraceae and the genus of Ficus which are native to Mediterranean climates, Southern parts of Asia and western parts of Africa.

Fig trees have lobed leaves with male and female flowers with smooth barks that have color range of between brown, white and gray depending on the cultivar planted.

Fig trees are grown in most parts of the world as edible fruits or for ornamental purposes with the most common ones being Black Mission fig, Chicago Hardy Fig, Kadota Figs and so on.

Edible figs can be eaten fresh or dried for later use. Edible figs can as well be used in making jams, jellies and desserts.

Figs have a rich history as it has been planted and used for several years. Fig trees were first grown in Rome with the first 25 varieties being grown then. They later spread to Asian climates and Mediterranean climates. There are over 600 cultivars of fig trees and they can be distinguished based on shape, size and fruit color. Figs were first brought to California in the 1520's by the missionaries with the most common variety being Mission Fig in California. Figs have been mentioned in the bible several times with many people believing it was the forbidden fruit.

GROWING FIG TREES

Figs have been used for religious purposes over the years by the Christians and Muslims to represent fertility and flourishing.

GROWING FIG TREES

Figs are packed with important nutritional components required in the body like proteins, vitamins, potassium, magnesium, fiber, carbs and copper.

Benefits

Figs may improve digestion

Figs contain high fiber contents which may help in improving digestion.

May improve the health of the heart

Figs extracts contain compounds which when consumed may help in improving the health of the heart.

May prevent cancer

Fig leaves may be infused to make fig tea and they may help to prevent cancer since they have anti-cancer properties.

GROWING FIG TREES

May improve skin health

Figs have high Vitamin C compounds which may help in improving the skin.

May improve blood sugar levels

Fig leaves may be infused to make fig tea which when may help in improving blood sugar levels when you take them on daily basis.

2 FIG TREES VARIETIES

FIG TREES VARIETIES

There are several varieties of fig trees which are mostly found in tropical climates. The most common fig trees are;

1. Black Mission Figs
2. Celeste Fig Trees
3. Common Fig Tree
4. Kadota Fig Trees
5. Moreton Bay Fig Trees
6. Chicago Hardy Fig Trees
7. Indian Banyan Fig Trees
8. Red Leaf Fig Trees
9. Weeping Fig Trees
10. Rubber Tree Fig Trees
11. Fiddleleaf Fig Trees
12. Chinese Banyan Fig Trees
13. Creeping Fig Trees

1. Black Mission Figs

Black Mission Figs are fig trees mostly found In hot and dry climates which produces black to purple fig fruits which have medium to large sizes. Black Mission figs have strawberry like flesh and sweet flavors.

Black Mission fig trees are common in California and can grow to a height of 25 feet when they are mature.

Black Mission fig trees produces two crops in a year in summer and fall.

2. Celeste Fig Trees

Celeste Fig Trees also referred to as sweet figs or sugar figs are fig trees mostly found in the southern parts of the United States. Celeste Fig

GROWING FIG TREES

Trees produce edible sweet fruits with high carbohydrates and the best thing about them is that they can be grown both indoors and outdoors.

Celeste Fig Trees perform well under full sunlight and well drained soils in order for them to produce healthy fruits.

3.   Common Fig Tree

Common Fig Tree are deciduous fig trees which are native to Mediterranean climates. They have white barks with lobed leaves and can grow to a height of between 12 to 25 feet when they are fully established. You should plant Common Fig trees between zones 9 to 11 under full sunlight.

Common Fig Tree are fig trees found in many stores due to their sweet edible fig fruits that have high nutritional components like Vitamins.

4. Kadota Fig Trees

Kadota Fig Trees are fig trees which perform well in cold climatic conditions and can grow to a height of 20 feet when fully established.

Kadota Fig Trees produce sweet fruits which can be used in making jellies and jams.

5. Moreton Bay Fig Trees

Moreton Bay Fig Trees also referred to as Australian Banyan fig tree are fig trees which are native to the eastern parts of Australia. Moreton Bay fig trees have large trunks with brown to grayish barks and leathery leaves.

GROWING FIG TREES

You can plant Moreton fig trees between zones 9 to 11 under full sunlight to partial shade.

6. Chicago Hardy Fig Trees

Chicago Hardy Fig Trees are hardy fig trees that can be grown between zones 6 to 11. Chicago Hardy Fig Trees have gray barks with silvery appearance and dark greenish leaves and fruits.

Chicago Hardy Fig trees can be grown both indoors and outdoors between zones 6 to 11 under full sunlight to partial shade.

7. Indian Banyan Fig Trees

Indian Banyan Fig Trees also referred to as Bengal figs are fig trees which are native to Asia and India tropical climates. Indian Banyan Fig trees can grow in holes of fully mature fig trees since they can easily absorb

moisture from the air. Banyan Fig trees have large trunks and grayish barks. They produce dark greenish leaves which have leathery appearance.

Banyan fig trees can grow to a height of 95 feet when they are fully established. You can grow Banyan fig trees under full sunlight between zones 9 to 12.

8. Red Leaf Fig Trees

Red Leaf Fig Trees also referred to as Cluster figs due to their ability to produce small fig fruits in clusters. Red Leaf Fig trees are native to the tropical climates of Australia and can grow to a height of 12 to 32 feet when fully established.

Red Leaf Fig trees should be planted between zones 9 to 11 under full sunlight to partial shade.

9. Weeping Fig Trees

Weeping Fig Trees are fig trees which are native to tropical climates of Australia and South Asia. Weeping Fig Trees have large trunks with gray barks and smooth leaf appearance.

GROWING FIG TREES

You should plant Weeping Fig Trees between zones 9 to 11 under full sunlight to partial shade. Fully established Weeping Fig trees can grow to a height of 55 feet.

10. Rubber Tree Fig Trees

Rubber Tree Fig are fig trees which are native to the tropical climates of Malaysia and India. Rubber Fig Trees have large trunks and oblong leaves that have shiny appearance.

Rubber Fig trees should be planted between 9 to 11 under full sunlight to partial shade.

11. Fiddleleaf Fig Trees

Fiddleleaf Fig Trees are fig trees that are native to Western Africa tropical climates.

GROWING FIG TREES

Fiddleleaf Fig trees produces huge leathery leaves and can grow to a height of 34 feet when they have fully established. Fiddleleaf Fig trees can be grown between zones 9 to 11 both indoors and outdoors.

12. Chinese Banyan Fig Trees

Chinese Banyan Fig Trees are fig trees which are mostly found in subtropical climates. They are native to Malaysia and India subtropical climates and have become invasive in Florida in the United States. Chinese Banyan fig trees produce oblong leaf shapes and small fig fruits.

GROWING FIG TREES

You should plant Chinese Banyan fig fruits under full sunlight to partial shade. Chinese Banyan fig trees can be planted between zones 9 to 11 with the trees reaching a height of 35 feet when they are fully established.

13. Creeping Fig Tree

Creeping Fig Tree are evergreen fig trees which are native to the tropical climates of East Asia. Creeping Fig Trees produce heart shaped greenish leaves.

Creeping Fig trees are mostly grown for ornamental purposes because they produces fruits which are not edible. Creeping fig trees require full sunlight and partial shade to grow and the good thing about them is that they are highly resistant to drought.

GROWING FIG TREES

Creeping Fig trees should be planted between zones 8 to 11 with the trees growing to heights of 14 feet when they are fully established.

3 FIG TREES GROWING REQUIREMENTS

FIG TREES GROWING REQUIREMENTS

Light and Temperatures

You should plant trees under full sunlight in order for them to produce more fruits. You should therefore ensure that they receive an average of 6 to 8 hours of sunlight per day. Fig trees use sunlight to absorb energy from the sun which helps in ensuring smooth flow of nutrients in the process called photosynthesis.

Fig trees perform well in warm climatic conditions although they may as well perform in cold climatic conditions.

GROWING FIG TREES

Soil

Fig trees can do well in most soil conditions but planting them in slightly acidic soils will be ideal for them. Acidic soils are good for fig trees as they can be able to absorb nutrients easily resulting in faster growth rates of fig trees.

Fig trees perform well in soils that are rich in organic matter and soils that can be able to conserve moisture contents. Organic matter will play a crucial role in ensuring that fig trees get the right nutrients like magnesium, phosphorus, nitrogen, calcium and potassium and in conserving the above nutrients. Figs generally require soil P.H that can range from 6.0 to 7.0 that is why I recommend that a soil test is first done to know the status of your soil. Soils that have low P.H can be improved by adding lime.

Propagation

Fig trees are propagated by cuttings method. Cuttings should be taken from healthy fig trees during the dormant period when the last frost has passed away. You can follow these simple steps to successfully propagate fig trees;

- Select healthy fig tree branch and cut an average of 10 inches in length.
- Place the cuttings in rooting hormone.
- Prepare potting mix and place the cuttings in the soil.
- Place the new plants in a warm and dry spot that can be able to receive an average of 6 to 8 hours of sunlight per day.
- Water the plants frequently so that the soils can become moist.
- Transplant the plants to individual containers when they get a set of four to five leaves.

GROWING FIG TREES

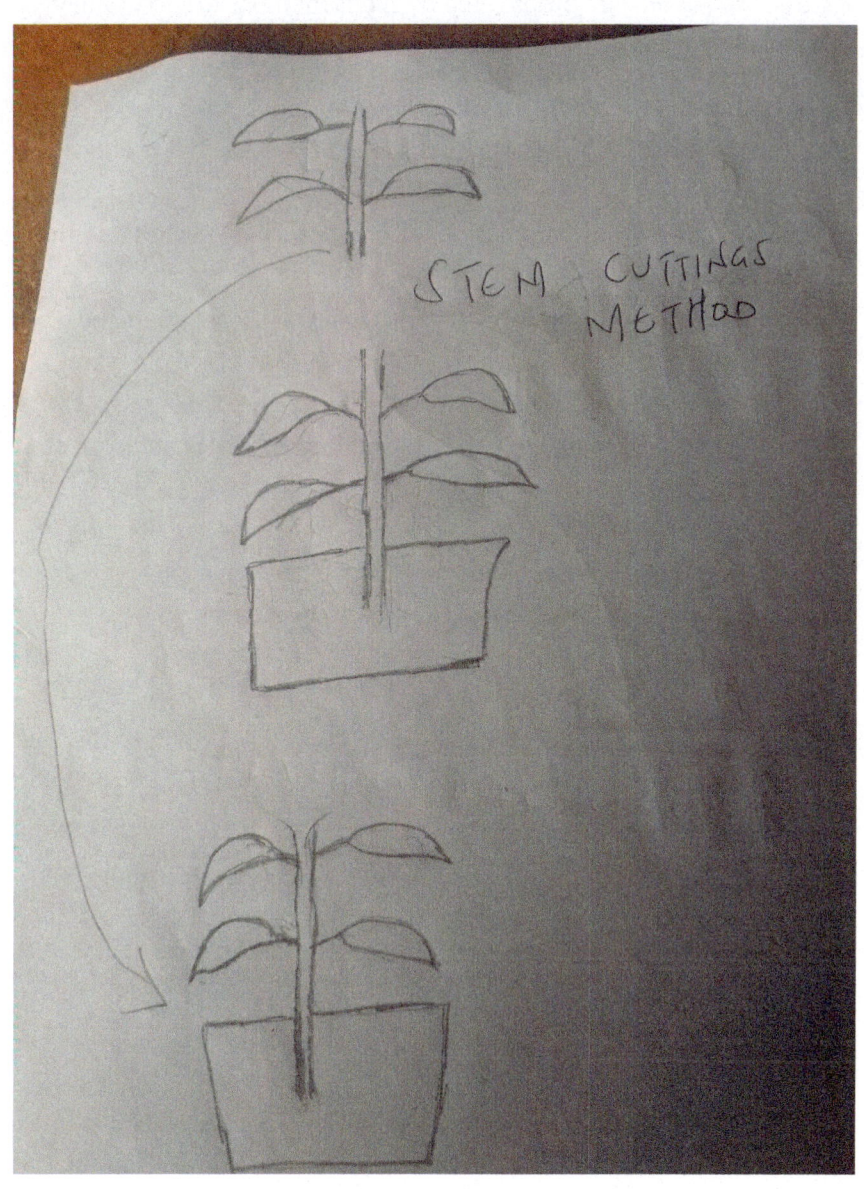

GROWING FIG TREES

Fig trees can as well be propagated by seeds method. To successfully propagate fig trees by seeds method you can follow these simple steps;

- Take seeds from healthy fig trees. You should take the seeds from female varieties since those are the ones that produces fruits.
- Cut the fig fruit into two pieces and remove the seeds and the fleshy pulp.
- Place the seeds in water to know which ones are good and which ones are not. You should use seeds that soak in water.
- Prepare potting soil and plant the seeds. The plants should receive an average of 6 to 8 hours of light per day and consistent water to retain the moisture content in the soil.
- Germination will occur after two to three weeks of planting.
- Transplant the new plants to individual containers or permanent field when they attain a set of four to five leaves.

GROWING FIG TREES

Planting

You should dig a hole size of 2 by 2 by 2 feet and then mix the top soil with 21 kgs of organic manure. You can then pre-fill the planting hole.

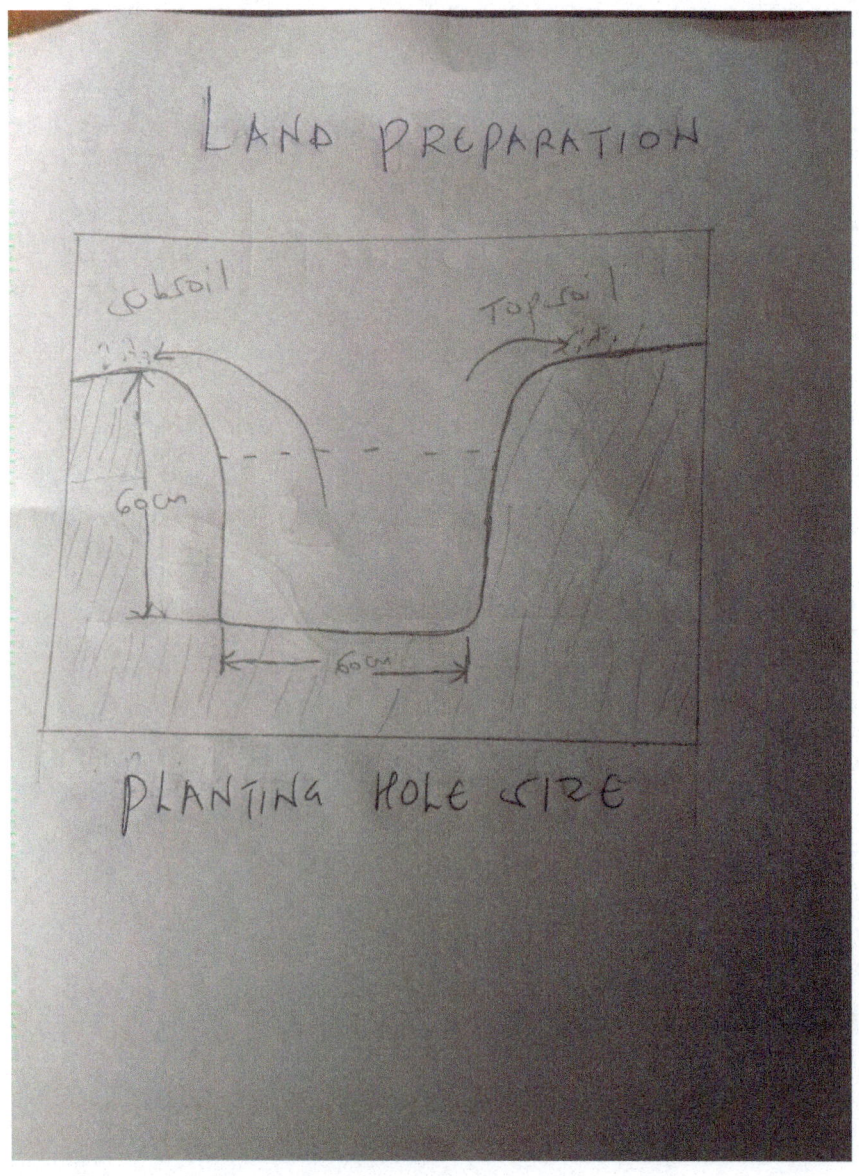

Fertilizer

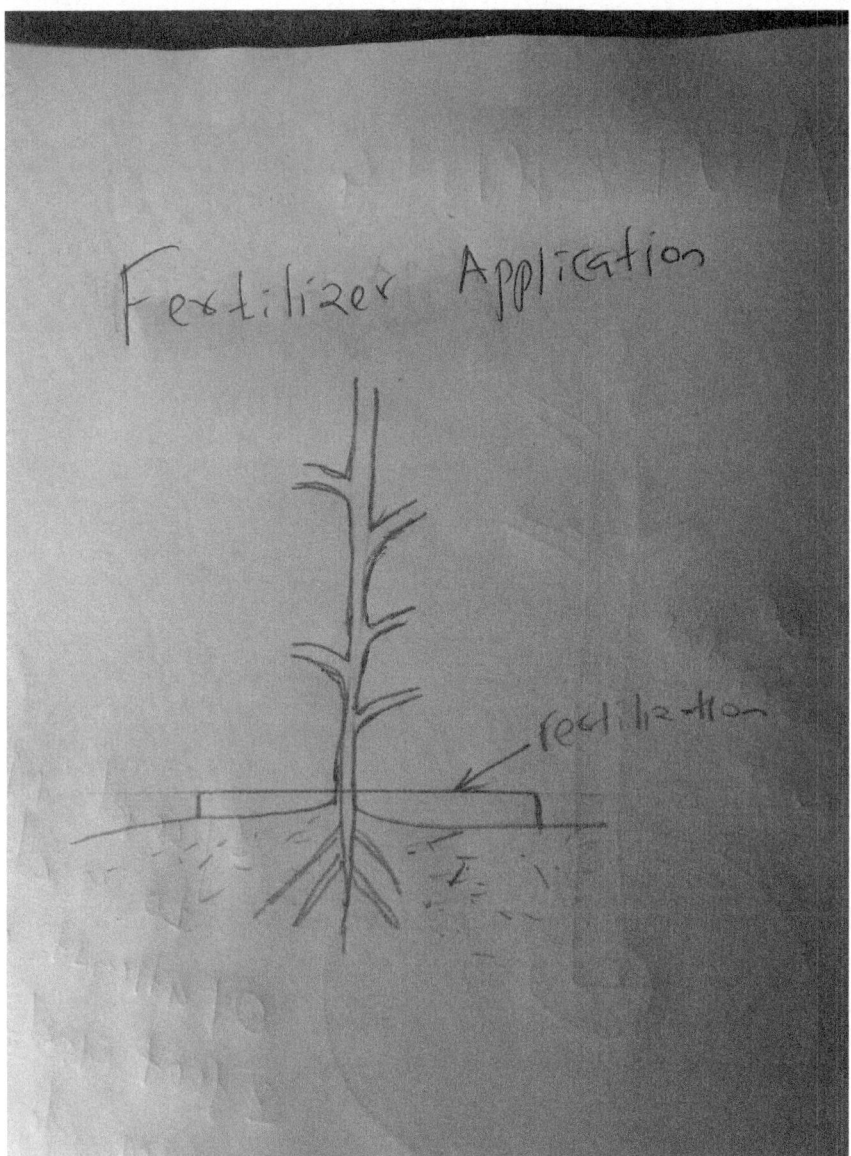

Fig trees require good fertilizers in order for them to produce abundant fruits. You should therefore ensure that fig trees get balanced fertilizer needs during their growing season in order for them to produce healthy crops. The best time to fertilize fig trees is during early spring so that they can be able to get the required nutrients during their active season.

Water

Fig trees require regular water needs in order for them to produce sweet figs. You should water fig trees frequently when they are newly planted so that they can be able to develop strong root systems.

Fig trees should not be overwatered as this may lead to poor growth rates of fig trees and infestation of diseases like Root rot.

Mulching

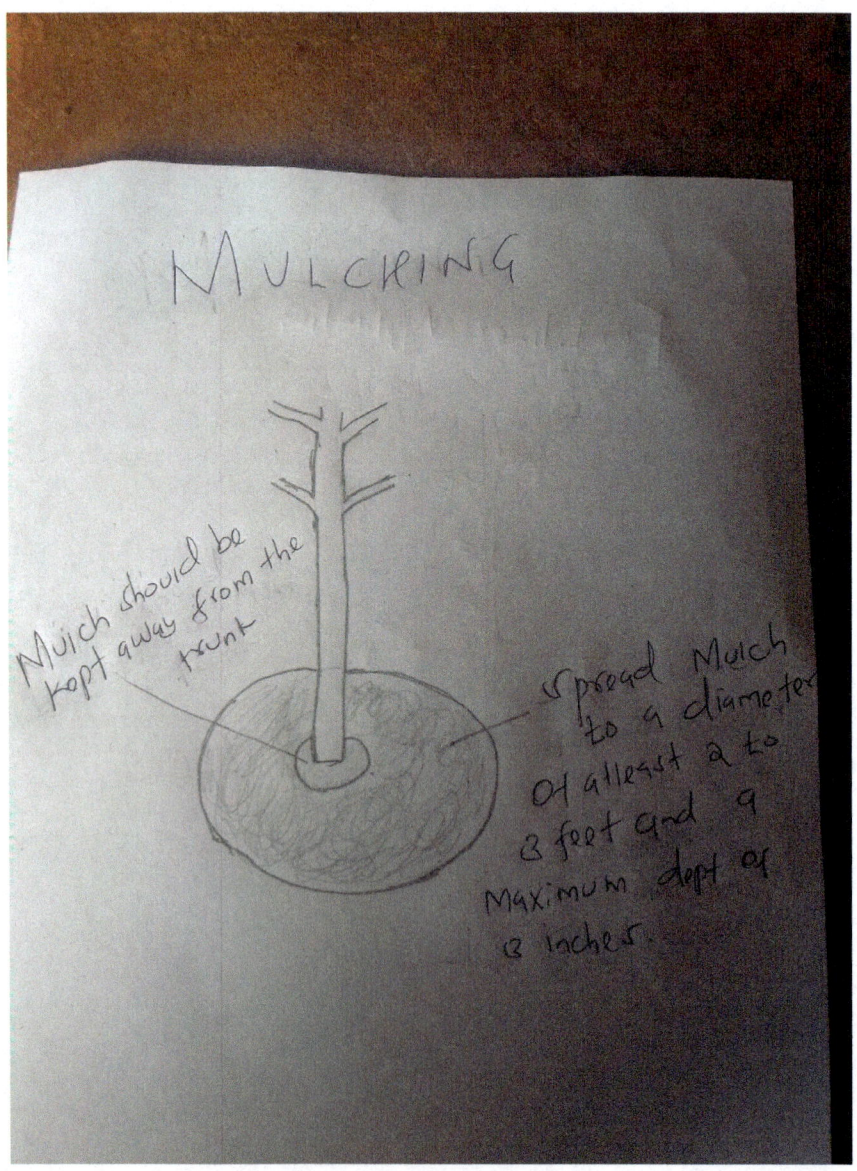

Fig trees require mulching around the tree trunks to protect them against soil erosion and to retain moisture content required for development of abundant fruits.

Repotting

Fig trees grown in containers require repotting and this can be done after every two to three years.

Repotting is crucial to figs planted in containers so that they can be able to get new nutrients required for their growth and to ensure that there is smooth air flow to the roots of the tree.

Pruning

GROWING FIG TREES

You should prune fig trees when they are dormant so that new and healthy growths can occur during their active season.

Pruning fig trees will also help in production of more healthy fruits in the subsequent years and in prevention of various diseases that may affect fig trees like cankers and leaf curl.

Harvesting

Fig fruits are ready for harvesting after two years of planting using cuttings method. Fig trees planted using seeds propagation method may take 3 to 4 years and the success rate may be minimal that is why I recommend planting fig trees using cuttings method. Figs that are grown outdoors between zones 5 to 7 will ripening between august to September whereas those planted between zones 8 to 11 will ripen in June.

You should harvest fig fruits when they have fully ripened and attained a soft skin appearance. Fully ripened fig fruits are very sweet and that is why birds and squirrels love them. You can cover your fruits with nets the moment they begin to ripen to avoid damage by the birds and squirrels.

GROWING FIG TREES

The right time to harvest figs will be based on the variety of figs planted, the zones in which they are planted and the fruit color. Ripened fig fruits will attain a full color of deep plum or yellow to green. Their sticky sugar sap may as well drop at the base of the fruit which can be an indicator that it is time to harvest your figs. You can harvest fig fruits by holding the fruit and lifting it up slowly as fully ripened figs will be easily detachable.

GROWING FIG TREES

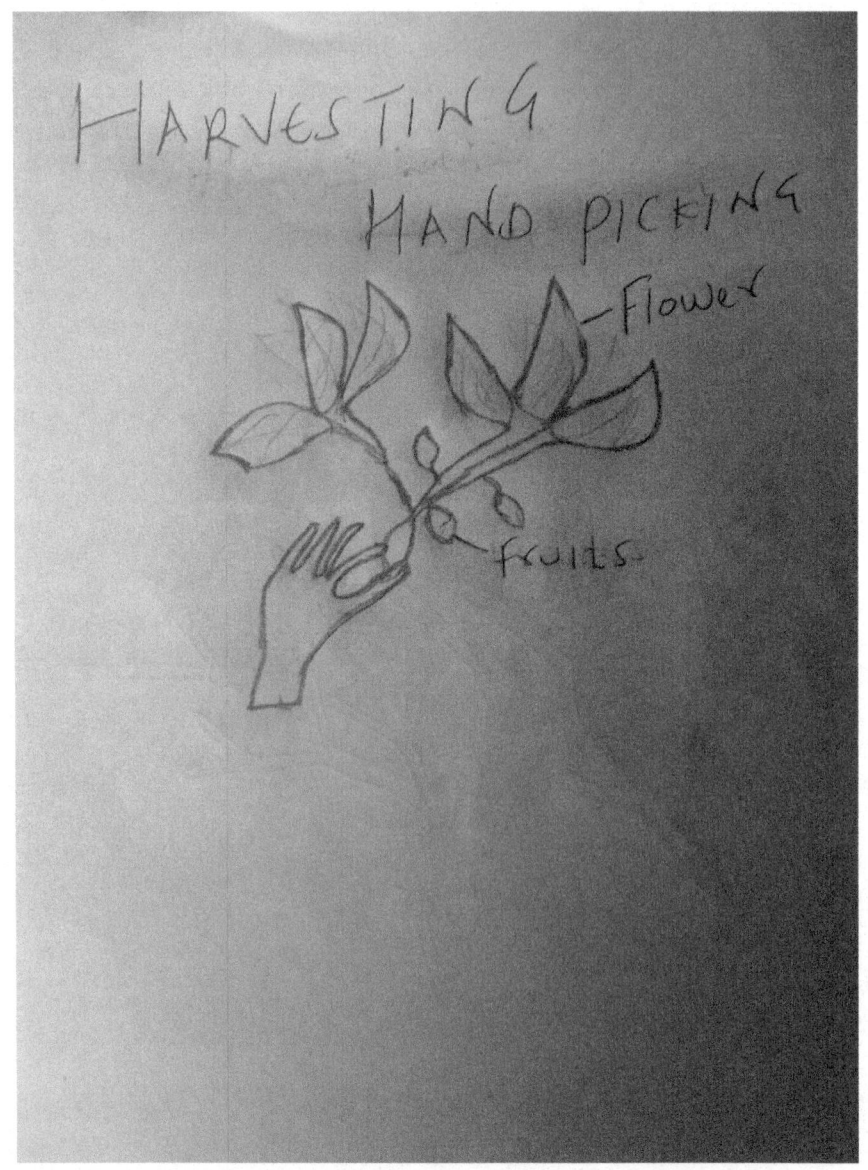

Post harvesting

Harvested figs have soft appearance and they can be eaten after they have been picked or kept in a refrigerator for about two to three days. You can as well dry them if you intend to keep them for several weeks.

4 POPULAR FIG TREES PESTS AND DISEASES

POPULAR FIG TREES PESTS AND DISEASES

Fig trees are not susceptible to pests and diseases when they are grown under right conditions. Pests and diseases mostly occur when fig trees are not planted under right soil and improper maintenance during their growing season. The most common pests and diseases that may likely affect fig trees are;

1. Root Knot Nematodes
2. Spider Mites
3. Scales
4. Fruit Flies
5. Rust
6. Mealybugs
7. Thrips
8. Anthracnose
9. Root Rot

1. Root Knot Nematodes

Root Knot Nematodes are soil borne diseases that are spread by infested seedlings or infested planting materials.

Root Knot Nematodes may cause yellowing of fig tree leaves, wilting and stunted growth rates of fig trees.

Root Knot Nematodes can be controlled by ensuring that you solarize your seedbeds for a span of 2 months and by ensuring that the planting area is kept free from weeds.

2. Spider Mites

Spider Mites are tiny insects which occur in colonies on the lower part of fig tree leaf surfaces. These tiny insects suck the cell sap content of fig leaves resulting in yellowing of the leaves and web formation on leaves.

Spider Mites can be controlled by keeping the planting area free from weeds and by uprooting infested fig parts to avoid further spread.

3. Scales

Scales are tiny brown to green insects which affect fig trees by sucking the sap from fig leaves resulting in stunted growth rates, dropping of fruits, leaf discoloration and eventual dropping of the leaves.

Scales can be prevented by conserving natural enemies like lacewings and parasitic wasps.

4. Fruit Flies

Fruit Flies are tiny insects which lay eggs on fig fruits the moment they begin to ripen resulting in cracks of the fruits that have star like shapes.

Fruit Flies can be controlled by ensuring that fig planting area is free from weeds or by using trap flies or nets the moment fig fruits begin to ripen.

5. Rust

Rust is a fungal disease which affects fig trees by forming brown spots on the lower part of the leaves.

Rust fungal disease can be controlled by keeping the planting area free from weeds and by spraying the blooms before they begin fruit formation.

6. Mealybugs

Mealybugs are tiny flat insects with soft bodies that affect fig trees by sucking the sap from their leaves and fruits resulting in yellowing of leaves and drying of the leaves.

Mealybugs can be controlled by ensuring that affected leaves and fruits are destroyed before they can spread out.

7.　Thrips

Thrips are slender and tiny insects which feed on small fig fruits resulting in silvery appearance on the affected parts and drying up of fig tree plant tissues.

Thrips can be controlled by keeping natural enemies like lacewings and predatory Thrips to keep them away.

8.　Anthracnose

Anthracnose is a fungal disease which is harmful to fig fruits when not controlled early.

Anthracnose may cause fig fruits to have dark brownish colors and dry spots resulting in improper development of the trees.

Anthracnose disease can be controlled by ensuring that the planting area is sanitized. Anthracnose can as well be treated by spraying them with fungicides like Mancozeb.

9. Root Rot

Root Rot is a fungal diseases which can affect fig trees when they are planted in soils that are poorly drained.

Root Rot may resulting in wilting of the trees and pale greenish color in affected leaves.

Root Rot may be controlled by uprooting affected fig trees and by ensuring that fig tree seeds are treated with hot water for 24 hours before propagating them.

ABOUT THE AUTHOR

Davies Cheruiyot is an agribusiness specialist with a degree in agribusiness. He turned to farming in 2015 to expand his knowledge on agriculture. He is the author of Growing Raspberries, Growing Dragon Fruits, Growing Strawberries and several other books

Printed in Great Britain
by Amazon